Introduction

There are three extraordinary, trailblazing women featured in this book.

Hürrem was born between 1502-1506.

Nur Jahan was born in 1577.

Lakshmibai was born in 1828.

At the times Hürrem, Nur Jahan and Lakshmibai lived, most women and girls were not treated the same way as men and boys. In some societies, it was the custom for girls to be married when they were quite young and to have fewer rights and less power than their husbands. Despite this, these girls grew into women who were brave and determined, and brought about great change.

Lakshmibai
The legend of Jhansi

This is the story of Lakshmibai, Queen of Jhansi – a name that would become legendary in India. Lakshimbai wasn't born a queen. In fact, her name was Manikarnika Tambe, and she was born in 1828 in a place called Varanasi in India. When she was four, her mother died, and her father raised her alone.

When Manikarnika turned 14, her father arranged for her to marry the **Maharaja** of Jhansi. His name was Gangadhar Rao. In this time and in this land, it was perfectly normal for girls to be married at the age of 14, and for marriages to be arranged. Manikarnika was excited to marry the Maharaja and start her new life as Queen of Jhansi.

The wedding took place in 1842. The most important people in Jhansi were gathered at the temple to celebrate the marriage. Manikarnika took a long, deep breath, aware that all eyes were on her. Everyone waited patiently for her to walk through the line of guests; some of the heavily-jewelled women cooled their faces with beautiful handmade fans.

They watched as Manikarnika took a small step forward, and then another and another behind her father, Moropant Tambe. Some of the men noted the pride in Moropant's face. He was a minister from Cawnpore Palace in the neighbouring kingdom. Moropant only worked for the royal family there, and yet it was his daughter who was marrying a maharaja.

Manikarnika's father had raised his daughter well after she'd lost her mother. Now, he was handing her in marriage to the Maharaja, who was waiting for her by the marriage fire, ready to walk around the flames seven times in a Hindu ceremony. This tradition would bind the groom and bride together forever.

Manikarnika's pace was slow under the weight of her bridal outfit. A red embroidered sari, covered in beads and gold thread, was draped around her body, and the sparkling jewels that hung from her ears, on her head and around her neck gleamed in the sunlight. She wasn't complaining though. Manikarnika was happy. Very happy. Today, she would not only become a wife, but a rani, a queen. The Rani of Jhansi.

When the ceremony was complete, Gangadhar Rao and Manikarnika stood before the people who had gathered to catch a glimpse of their new queen.

"I thank you for your good wishes on my marriage," the Maharaja began. "The name given to my wife at birth was Manikarnika. It's a beautiful name but we, the people of Jhansi, will give our queen a new name to reflect the good fortune she has brought on us. From this day on, she will be known as Lakshmibai.

Oh, people of Jhansi, bow before your queen, Rani Lakshmibai."

The crowd erupted into cheers, and Lakshmibai felt an overwhelming surge of love for her new people. They had accepted her with open arms, and in her heart she made a silent promise to devote her life to the people of Jhansi.

Rani Lakshmibai settled into her new home and the years passed. She was happy with the Maharaja and watched closely as he ruled his kingdom. For a long time, they both wished for a child. Nine years after their marriage, when Lakshmibai was 23 years old, she had a beautiful baby boy. When she held the little bundle in her arms for the first time, Lakshmibai felt a burst of love that she'd never felt before. The Maharaja and Rani named their baby son Damodar, and spent all their time cuddling and playing with him.

Rani Lakshmibai thought she would be happy forever, as long as she had her husband and son by her side. Unfortunately, her happiness didn't last. On an overcast day, the baby prince breathed his last breath, and shut his eyes forever. The grief that Rani Lakshmibai felt was overwhelming. There was a pain inside her like she'd never known before. It seemed like a sharp tool had cut her heart out and she thought she would never heal from the wound.

This was not the only tragedy to befall Rani Lakshmibai. The Maharaja soon fell ill. Lakshmibai sat by his bedside and they both cried over their lost son. When their tears had dried, the Maharaja took Lakshmibai's hand and entwined his fingers with hers.

"You must be strong now," he whispered. "I am too ill to rule, and you must take my place."

"How can I?" Rani Lakshmibai gasped. "I'm just a woman."

"You are a rani," he said. "The Rani of Jhansi, and you must protect my people and lead them."

"Who am I protecting them from?" Rani Lakshmibai asked, feeling confused.

"Those who have sailed over large seas to take our land," the Maharaja mumbled. His voice became faint, and his hand fell back on the bed. He was so weak that even talking exhausted him.

Rani Lakshmibai brushed his hair off his forehead. "Sleep, my love," she said.

She, however, did not sleep that night. What did the Maharaja mean when he said Jhansi needed protecting? She didn't have to wait long to find out. The next day the Dewan, the Prime Minister of Jhansi, came to see her.

"Rani Lakshmibai," the Dewan began, with his head bent respectfully. "I'm your humble servant, and I must share the most distressing news with you."

"Nothing can be more distressing than losing my son," Rani Lakshmibai whispered. "Nothing."

"You are *still* a mother," the Dewan said, raising his eyes to meet hers. "As Rani, you are a mother to the people in this kingdom. And you must protect them."

Rani Lakshmibai sat up in her chair, intrigued. The Dewan was repeating the Maharaja's words. "I need you to explain it all to me," she said. "What do you mean by 'protect them'?"

The Dewan cleared his throat. "As you know, the first ship that sailed from England to our lands in 1608 belonged to the East India Company. The ship was called *Red Dragon*, and its merchants came to buy and sell goods. But as the years passed, the East India Company's desire for power and wealth grew. Now, 200 years later, they've taken over many kingdoms in India with their private army of soldiers. The East India Company is run by the Governor General of India, Lord Dalhousie. They are supported by the British Government."

Rani Lakshmibai nodded gravely. "Indeed, I've heard of Lord Dalhousie."

"Lord Dalhousie claims the kingdom of Jhansi now belongs to the East India Company," the Dewan continued.

Rani Lakshmibai had never heard anything so preposterous. "Why does he think that?"

"The East India Company follows a law called the Doctrine of Lapse," the Dewan explained. "It means that the kingdom of Jhansi must be handed over to them as the Maharaja has no heir to inherit the throne."

Rani Lakshmibai froze in her seat. "The Maharaja and I will have more children," she said stiffly.

The Dewan lowered his eyes. "Your Royal Highness, with all due respect, the Maharaja is ill. You know it. I know it. Everyone in Jhansi knows it and all the leaders of the East India Company know it too. It's not possible for the Maharaja to have any more children. He's not long for this world."

Words failed Rani Lakshmibai. If she was honest, she did know this, but hearing the words said aloud by the Dewan made their situation starkly real. And now, the East India Company wanted to take away her kingdom.

"Rani Lakshmibai," the Dewan said, eyes still lowered. "You must take steps to secure your throne."

"How?" she asked.

"You must adopt a child related to the royal family and declare him to be your official heir."

"Who?"

"Anand Rao is the four-year-old son of the Maharaja's cousin. He must become the official heir to the throne to stop the East India Company from taking our kingdom."

For the first time since her baby son died, Rani Lakshmibai felt a rush of blood in her veins. She placed her feet on the floor and rose. "Make the arrangements, Dewan Saheb," she ordered. "We must save Jhansi from the clutches of the East India Company."

Rani Lakshmibai chose to visit Anand Rao rather than have him brought to the palace. She believed it would be much better for the boy to meet her in his familiar surroundings. If he was going to be her son and heir to Jhansi, then he needed to come willingly.

The Dewan organised a small escort to the boy's home. Sitting in the shade of a large banyan tree, Rani Lakshmibai waited for Anand Rao to be brought to her. It was his mother who led him out, and it was obvious that he'd been told of this meeting because he clutched her hand as if he would never let go.

When Rani Lakshmibai rose to her feet, the boy hid behind his mother's sari. "I don't want to go with you," Anand Rao blurted out. "I want to stay with my mother."

Rani Lakshmibai knelt so that she could look into the boy's large, brown eyes. He reminded her of a deer that had been trapped by hunters.

"I'm not here to take you anywhere," she said. "I'm here to ask if you would like to ride horses with me."

The fear in Anand Rao's eyes faded and he visibly relaxed. "You can ride horses?" There was awe in his voice.

"I can."

"But you're a woman."

"Indeed, I am," Rani Lakshmibai agreed, with a small smile.

Anand looked impressed, but he didn't let go of his mother's hand.

Rani Lakshmibai sat back down on the chair. "I own a horse called Sarangi. He's a glorious, strong stallion, and he can gallop as fast as the wind. When I ride him, it's like I'm flying."

Anand Rao let go of his mother's hand and stepped forward.

"Would you like to meet Sarangi?" Rani Lakshmibai asked.

Anand Rao nodded.

"Well, you shall have to come to the palace because Sarangi lives there, in the stables," Rani Lakshmibai said.

"What about my mother and father?" Anand Rao asked.

"They can come too," she promised.

It didn't take long for Anand Rao to settle into the palace. He loved to ride Sarangi with Rani Lakshmibai. He felt like he was the maharaja of the world when he was seated up on the saddle with her.

One morning, Rani Lakshmibai asked Anand Rao a question as they rode in the morning light. "Would you like to live with me in the palace forever?"

"What about my mother?"

"You can see her anytime you want," Rani Lakshmibai promised. "I wouldn't separate a mother from her son."

They were both silent for a while, and then Rani Lakshmibai said, "I had a son once, but he died."

"That's very sad," Anand said.

"Yes, it was very, very sad, but now I need a new son to sit with me on the throne," Rani Lakshmibai admitted. "I'd like that to be you."

Anand Rao thought about it. "OK, I'll be your son."

The Dewan worked tirelessly to arrange the adoption ceremony. It was vital that all the neighbouring royals and members of the East India Company witnessed the Maharaja and Rani adopt Anand Rao, and know he was not just any boy, but one that had royal blood. They gave him a new name: Damodar – the name they'd given their first child.

The day of the adoption ceremony arrived, and Anand Rao sat between the Maharaja and Rani, in front of hundreds of guests. They gave the young prince his new name and when the ceremony was over, the Maharaja struggled to his feet and held up the boy's hand to the crowd.

"My son, Prince Damodar, heir to the kingdom of Jhansi," he declared.

The crowd erupted into cheers and Rani Lakshmibai bent down so that she could whisper in her new son's ear. "Wave to your people, Prince Damodar."

Damodar raised a hand and waved to the crowd, and they cheered for him even more.

Rani Lakshmibai breathed a sigh of relief. Jhansi was safe from the greedy hands of the East India Company. This land belonged to the people of Jhansi. They'd lived on it for a thousand years and there was no way they were going to give it up.

The joy of the adoption was replaced with tears the next day. The Maharaja died in his bed and all the people of Jhansi wept for him.

Rani Lakshmibai threw herself into running the kingdom. She made sure the soldiers trained hard, the poor were fed and the orphans looked after. The rest of her time was spent with Damodar, and the young prince was bright and eager to please.

Rani Lakshmibai was still a young woman, but she dedicated her time to training Damodar to take over the kingdom when she was gone. Jhansi needed a protector, and he was its future.

A year after the Maharaja died, the Dewan asked to speak to the Rani alone.

Rani Lakshmibai sent Damodar to play with his friends in the courtyard. Raising her chin, she steeled herself for his words, but he looked at her as if he didn't know what to say.

"What is it?" Rani Lakshmibai demanded. "Why do you look as if the sky is about to fall in?"

"Indeed, the sky is about to fall in on top of us," the Dewan agreed.

"Tell me!" Rani Lakshmibai commanded.

"Lord Dalhousie lives in faraway Calcutta and he's a very busy man who has to make decisions on many important matters. It's for this reason that it's taken him several months to address the adoption of Prince Damodar. I have been told that now, after careful consideration, he can't accept the new prince as the rightful heir to Jhansi."

Rani Lakshmibai's mouth fell open with surprise. "He can't do that," she spat. "Prince Damodar was declared to be my son and official heir to Jhansi. The world came to witness it, and the ceremony was blessed by all the priests."

"That's all very well," the Dewan said. "But who will reason with Dalhousie?"

"I will!" Rani Lakshmibai declared.

Much to Rani Lakshmibai's indignation, she was not successful. Lord Dalhousie refused to listen to her argument and ordered his troops to attack if Jhansi wasn't handed to him. Despite her fury, Rani Lakshmibai was helpless. Her soldiers couldn't win against the East India Company's army, which had 250,000 soldiers. She had no choice but to hand over Jhansi.

On the day of the handover, Rani Lakshmibai nodded to the Dewan to pass her the keys to the treasury and Jhansi Fort to the British superintendent, Captain Skene. She was permitted to stay on at the palace with a small number of bodyguards and servants, but she was no longer the ruler of Jhansi.

Three years passed and by 1857 Damodar had grown into a strong eight-year-old boy under the watchful eye of Rani Lakshmibai. She showered him with love and made sure he received the training and education that was expected of all royal princes. Damodar was not the only one who was instructed in horse-riding and sword-fighting. Rani Lakshmibai insisted that her women companions were given the same lessons. She believed it was vital that her people had the skills to fight Lord Dalhousie's army. In her heart, she still carried the hope that one day she would take back Jhansi from the East India Company and rule it again.

The year 1857 was one of turmoil in most of the kingdoms in India. Rani Lakshmibai heard stories that travelled from other places. The East India Company had become increasingly arrogant in their rule over the Indians; they had little respect for tradition, and were causing resentment and rebellion. In the northern city of Delhi, which had been the capital of the **Mughal Empire**, the Mughal Emperor, Bahadur Shah Zafar II, had been declared Emperor of the whole of India after his peoples' victory over the East India Company soldiers.

Rani Lakshmibai waited anxiously with the Dewan by her side. They both knew it was only a matter of time before the rebels fighting against the East India Company found their way to Jhansi. Rebellions always brought violence, and Rani Lakshmibai didn't want innocent people to be killed in her land.

It was early in the morning when the Dewan rushed to Rani Lakshmibai with news. "The rebels have arrived in Jhansi and they're urging the local people to join their cause. They are almost at the gates of Jhansi Fort."

Rani Lakshmibai frowned. Captain Skene and his soldiers from the East India Company were at the fort. They were her enemies, but the soldiers' families were also there. Women and children.

Rani Lakshmibai scraped back her chair and walked to the window. She gazed down at the courtyard below where Damodar was learning to fight with his wooden sword. The British children in the fort were his age and younger. They would be put in terrible danger if the rebels sparked a riot.

"I want you to send messengers to Captain Skene. They are to inform him of the secret tunnel that runs from the fort to this palace. He should send the women and children out of harm's way. I will make sure they escape Jhansi to a safer place."

The Dewan gazed at Rani Lakshmibai in amazement. "But Rani Lakshmibai, if the rebels find out that you helped the British, they will turn against you."

Rani Lakshmibai raised her chin in defiance. "I will not have the blood of innocent women and children on my hands. They can't be expected to pay for the decisions the East India Company have made."

"Very well," the Dewan said, bowing his head.

The plan worked. That night, British women and children rushed through the tunnel from the fort to the palace. Some of the children were afraid, but Rani Lakshmibai and her companions comforted them.

"Hush," Rani Lakshmibai soothed. "You're safe now."

Unfortunately, Captain Skene didn't send all the families. Some of the women wanted to stay behind with their soldier husbands, and the captain allowed it. Now, with the rebels banging on the fort gates, the captain decided that everyone who remained should leave on horseback and in carriages. If the rebels wanted the fort, they could have it for now. He had no doubt in his mind that the East India Company would come back another day to reclaim it.

The first officer was not so keen on leaving through the main gates. "Perhaps we should exit through the tunnel as well, sir."

"Don't be ridiculous!" Captain Skene snapped. "We shall leave with dignity through the baying mob. There is no way we are going to flee like rats."

The first officer's face fell, but he could not disobey an order. "Very well, sir."

The small group didn't get very far. The rebels stopped them just by the gates.

"You can't leave," the chief rebel stated calmly.

"We have women and children with us," Captain Skene retorted. "Out of the way!"

"Still so arrogant," the rebel snarled. "You come to our land and think you can rule us because you have guns and soldiers. Well, we can fight back too, and today we'll teach you a lesson."

Captain Skene realised his mistake and softened his voice. "Look, old chap, let us leave and I promise you that we'll never return to Jhansi again."

"We don't believe you," the rebel said. "If we let you go now, you'll return with bigger numbers. I think, good sir, it's a case of you or us. We choose us."

Rani Lakshmibai was still in her palace when news of the attack reached her. Running to her horse, she swung into the saddle and galloped down to the fort. Tears gathered in her eyes when she saw the sight before her.

"Any survivors at all?" Rani Lakshmibai called out.

"None!" someone shouted back.

Rani Lakshmibai made up her mind. She spun her horse around and raced back to the palace.

"Dewan – Saheb," she shouted, as she marched into the palace. "I need you to send word to the East India Company. There's no one left in charge here; therefore, I'm taking control again. I'm taking Jhansi back."

Rani Lakshmibai took possession of the fort and established order over Jhansi. The East India Company, however, did not leave her in peace.

Only months later, in March 1858, the East India Company marched a huge number of soldiers to Jhansi and demanded that Rani Lakshmibai surrender the kingdom again.

Rani Lakshmibai refused. She wasn't going to give up without a fight this time. She'd saved many of the British women and children, and she'd imposed peace. Why then would the East India Company still want her to surrender?

On the eve of battle, she stood before her people with Prince Damodar and her companions by her side. Each of the women was dressed for battle with their hair tucked under turbans and swords gleaming by their sides.

"We will fight for our land, each and every one of us!" Rani Lakshmibai gave the war cry. "It's a question of honour and justice. Jhansi belongs to us and only we will rule it."

The crowds cheered: "Long live Rani Lakshmibai. Victory to Jhansi!"

The battle was long and hard, and the people of Jhansi fought till the very end.

When it was clear that they couldn't win, Rani Lakshmibai's companions urged her to retreat. But she believed it was more important to fight another day. Rani Lakshmibai rode back to the palace and grabbed Damodar. She swung him behind her in the saddle and galloped as fast as she could away from her beloved Jhansi. She rode continuously for 24 hours and reached a town called Kalpi, where other Indian rulers and their followers had gathered against the East India Company's army.

This was their land, and the rulers were going to make a final stand. This was the First War of Independence.

Without their queen to defend it, the kingdom of Jhansi fell. It was robbed of its riches and then destroyed by the East India Company.

For the next three months, Rani Lakshmibai fought alongside the other Indian rulers and their armies. She handed Damodar to her most trusted companions for safekeeping and rode her horse into battle. The East India Company's troops outnumbered the Indian soldiers and, no matter how bravely the Indians fought, they couldn't beat the larger army.

On 18th June 1858, Rani Lakshmibai was killed on the battlefield defending the kingdom of Gwalior.

Rani Lakshmibai's surviving women companions and followers fled into the jungle with Prince Damodar. After a few years, the British government awarded him a small amount of money for the loss of his kingdom. Appalled by the way the East India Company had behaved in India, the British government also shut down the company and transferred control of India to the British Crown.

Rani Lakshmibai was one of the first to take a stand for freedom, and her actions helped to end the East India Company. The fight for complete freedom was continued by others who came after her and Britain ended its rule of India in 1947.

Hürrem
The maiden from Old Russia

This is the story of a young girl's journey from poverty and hardship, to the throne of the Ottoman Empire. The rise of this queen is impressive, but little could she have known how her life would turn out when she arrived in a strange, new land …

Known first as Roxelana, meaning "maiden from Old Russia", she was taken from her home around 1520 and brought to modern day Turkey as a slave. Over many years, Roxelana became one of the land's most influential women, and known as Hürrem, or "the joyful one". Inspired by her own struggles, she would go on to build hospitals and schools to help others.

Roxelana's feet ached. She didn't think she could take another step on the hard, rocky ground but the tug of the rope that tied her wrists together pulled her forwards.

Her feet were bruised and she stumbled; she would have fallen flat on her face had it not been for the woman directly in front of her.

"Watch it," the woman hissed over her shoulder.

"Sorry," Roxelana mumbled. "I'm just so tired."

The woman's face softened. "I'm Daryna," she said. "I heard those men call you Roxelana. Why?"

"It means 'maiden from Old Russia'," the girl muttered.

"Roxelana," Daryna repeated. "What's your real name?"

The girl jutted her chin, unwilling to share the name that belonged to someone who was free. She no longer had her freedom so what was the point?

"Just call me Roxelana," she uttered through stiff lips, thinking of her homeland. She'd been taken away weeks ago by slavers, and she wondered if her parents were still looking for her in their village near the city of Kyiv.

"Very well, Roxelana," Daryna said. "You're young and strong, you will be OK. Look at me. I'm 50. I'm not going to be much use here."

Roxelana stared at Daryna. The woman hadn't uttered a single word since they'd been tied by a long rope in a line two days ago. Now she was blabbering away. It was like a dam had broken and she couldn't stop.

"May a colony of ants crawl up the trousers of these men and bite their legs from now until the end of time for bringing me here," Daryna continued in a bitter voice.

"I'm sorry," Roxelana muttered, thinking of her own sadness. The first, second and third days had been the hardest. On the fourth day, she'd decided to accept her fate. She'd overheard the men talking; they were all travelling to the capital of the Ottoman Empire, to a city called **Constantinople**. Roxelana had heard it was the richest and grandest of all the cities in the world.

After months of travel on the road and then by ship across a sea, it felt like they were heading for the sun itself, with each day hotter than the last.

When they finally arrived in the wondrous city of Constantinople, she drank in the sight before her. The streets and bazaars were filled with all sorts of goods, and the people looked like they came from different parts of the world and were all happy to be living together in peace.

It seemed that every citizen was free to be whoever they wanted to be. Well, the free citizens, and not those like her who had been brought here to work.

During their time together, Roxelana grew close to Daryna. The journey East had been perilous and they'd supported each other on the road and then on a ship when a storm had threatened to toss them overboard. The woman and the young girl from Old Russia had clung to each other and lain flat on the ship's deck as the salty sea drenched them with powerful waves. Roxelana knew the day she would be separated from her friend was coming and she dreaded it. She had no one in the world except Daryna and the thought of being all alone in a strange city terrified her.

The day of their separation dawned bright. Daryna hugged Roxelana tightly.

"You be a brave girl now," Daryna whispered in her ear. "Who knows? Maybe we'll see each other again."

"Why are you being taken to the Grand Bazaar?" Roxelana asked.

"Because that is where I'll be chosen for a new home to work in," Daryna replied, releasing her.

Roxelana flung her arms around Daryna again for a final time. "Thank you for everything," she said, as her friend left the carriage. "I will see you again one day, I promise."

An hour later, the carriage stopped again and Roxelana was ordered to get out. She stared up in awe at her surroundings. She was standing in the courtyard of the grandest palace she had ever seen.

"What is this place?"

"The royal palace," her captor replied. "It's the main residence of Sultan Suleyman. This is the courtyard for the women's quarter."

Roxelana was led through the courtyard up to the doors of her new home.

"I bid you goodbye," he said. "I'm not permitted to go further inside. Only the men of the Sultan's family are allowed in."

Roxelana felt overwhelmed to be standing in the Sultan's palace. She'd never been anywhere so grand and colourful. The walls were covered in geometric patterned tiles in white and blue, and the windows were made of stained glass with red and green floral designs. She could see a lush garden full of pink roses ahead. All of a sudden, she missed the simplicity of her small family home in her little village. She was from Old Russia where it was cold, and everything was familiar. How would she live here? How would she be treated?

Suddenly, Roxelana heard a voice behind her. "Who are you?"

Startled, she spun around and stared at a middle-aged woman. "Roxelana," she mumbled.

"Eyes down," the woman snapped.

Roxelana lowered her gaze and was as still as a statue.

The woman stepped forward and grasped a lock of Roxelana's hair. "Dull and dry," she muttered, and then tilted Roxelana's chin up with her fingers. A crease appeared between her brows, expressing her disapproval. "Too much time in the sun."

Roxelana bit her lip. How could she explain that she had not been offered a veil to protect her from the sun's beams while she was held prisoner?

"We'll scrub you up and have you looking like a girl from the east," the woman said. "I'm Fatima and here, in the women's quarters, you'll do as I say."

A day later, Roxelana stared at her reflection in the clear fountain water. The scrubs and oils that had been rubbed onto her skin had transformed her into someone she didn't recognise.

"Beautiful," Fatima complimented. "Now we must improve your intellect. You'll learn to read, write and speak Arabic, Greek, Latin, Turkish and Persian. Education is important in the women's quarters."

Weeks passed and Roxelana slowly became accustomed to living in the Sultan's palace. There were about 300 people who worked in the quarter for the royal women. Roxelana got on with everyone, as she was kind and helpful to all.

One evening, as Roxelana walked through the garden, a voice greeted her from behind. "Hello."

Roxelana turned around and immediately lowered her eyes. The voice belonged to Sultan Suleyman. She'd seen him from afar when he visited his mother, the **Queen Mother** Hafsa, in the women's quarters, but this was the first time that she'd ever been addressed by him.

"What's your name?" the Sultan asked.

"Roxelana," she mumbled, her eyes still on the floor.

"Look at me," he commanded.

Roxelana obeyed.

"I shall call you Hürrem," he said. "It means the joyful one."

The Sultan visited Hürrem nearly every day, and he fell in love with her. Whenever he had to leave Constantinople, he wrote her letters that were filled with poetry, and she wrote back telling him how much she missed him.

Hürrem was happy in the women's quarters. Her position rose among the other women, and the servants and assistants obeyed her. However, her closeness with the Sultan meant that some of the other women grew jealous. Sometimes they made unkind remarks and left her out of their discussions and fun. She was happy with Suleyman but sometimes she wished that she had a friend that she could trust completely. And that's when Daryna's name popped into her head. That evening, Hürrem found the courage to ask the Sultan for a favour.

"Anything for you," Suleyman replied.

"On my journey here, I had a companion," Hürrem explained. "Her name was Daryna, and she was like a mother figure to me. I would be most grateful if she could be by my side."

"That is all?" Suleyman asked, with a chuckle. "I thought you were going to ask me for the moon and stars."

Hürrem smiled.

"Your wish is my command," Suleyman promised. "Daryna, if she is alive, will be with you by tomorrow."

True to his word, Daryna walked through the gates of the courtyard before nightfall the next day. She was carrying a small bundle under her arm and looking around in awe.

"Daryna!" Hürrem cried in joy, running through the courtyard and flinging her arms around her old friend. "I'm so happy to see you."

"Roxelana, let me look at you," Daryna said, stepping back.

"I'm known as Hürrem now." She linked her arm through Daryna's. "You shall live with me."

"And do what?" Daryna asked.

"Be by my side," Hürrem replied. "You'll be my companion."

Daryna settled into the palace and was by Hürrem's side when she gave birth to the Sultan's son. They named him Mehmed. As the years went on, Hürrem and the Sultan had another four sons and one daughter. Suleyman wanted nothing more than to marry her, but he knew he couldn't place the rank of a wife from Old Russia above the Queen Mother Hafsa.

When Hafsa died, the path was finally clear for Suleyman to marry Hürrem. She could now occupy the highest position of a woman in the Ottoman Empire.

Many in the palace and the other grand houses of Constantinople were against the marriage. Hürrem wasn't an Ottoman. She was an outsider who had no good family to support her. How could the Sultan marry such a woman?

Sultan Suleyman didn't listen to their grumblings. He loved Hürrem and wanted her by his side as his empress. He also wanted their firstborn son to be his heir and rule after him.

He was the Sultan and his word was law.

Hürrem and the Sultan's wedding was a grand affair. Celebrations rang out in Constantinople's streets and sweets were distributed to the gathering crowds. Ordinary people were happy for the beautiful couple, although there were a few bitter faces from the rich, who didn't approve.

Once she became the Empress, Hürrem didn't want to forget the people who were less fortunate than her. She remembered that she had been one of them once.

She ordered the **Haseki** Sultan Complex to be built, which included a school and a soup kitchen for the poor. The Haseki Hürrem Sultan Hospital was the first one built especially for women, and others in need. Hürrem also had public bath houses built so that everyone had access to water for washing.

The Sultan was often away on **military campaigns** across Europe and the Middle East, but he never forgot about Hürrem while he was managing his large empire. Suleyman and Hürrem wrote many letters to each other, filled with poems.

Hürrem tore open the seal to the latest letter and her eyes absorbed the words. When she finished, she leant back with a smile, hugging the letter to her chest. "He wrote another poem for me."

Daryna smiled. "He's far away fighting in a battle, he's known as Suleyman the Magnificent, and yet he takes the time to write poetry to you."

"He does," Hürrem admitted.

"You both have a special bond; your firstborn son Mehmed should become the Sultan's heir."

Hürrem looked up in surprise. "Suleyman has another son called Mustafa who was born before we met," she said. "The people favour him."

Daryna sighed. "It is you who is the haseki, Empress. Your son should be the next sultan."

Hürrem thought of Mehmed – he was 22 years old, and a fine young man. Maybe Daryna was right. Maybe Mehmed should become the sultan. But it was not to be.

The setting sun had turned the sky into streaks of red and orange flame when the door to Hürrem's rooms swung open.

Normally, Suleyman strode in with a sword jangling by his side and a huge smile on his face; he was always pleased to see Hürrem. Today, however, Suleyman's steps were heavy and slow. His shoulders were stooped as if he carried the weight of the world on them.

Hürrem jumped to her feet and ran to him. "What is it? Tell me!" she cried.

Suleyman's eyes shone with tears. Hürrem had rarely ever seen him cry. He was Suleyman the Magnificent who ruled as far as the eye could see!

"Tell me, please," Hürrem pleaded, fear moving through her body like a whirlwind.

"It is our son, Mehmed," Suleyman said gravely. "I've received the terrible news that he became ill and died."

"What? No!" Hürrem's hands flew to her mouth.

"I'm afraid it is true."

Hürrem's legs gave way from under her and she crumpled to the floor. Mehmed was the governor of Manisa, and he'd died far away from her. What if he'd cried for his mother in his pain? She hadn't been there for him.

Suleyman picked her up and carried her to a bench. There they sat together and cried for their firstborn son.

Now that Mehmed was gone, Hürrem worried about her remaining three sons.

Unlike in Europe, the firstborn son didn't automatically become the heir. The son who wanted to be the sultan had to fight his brothers and half-brothers for the throne. Suleyman was the father of eight sons and three of them had died when they were children. Mehmed was the fourth son to die. Hürrem knew her three remaining sons, Selim, Bayezid and Cihangir, would fight for the throne, as would Suleyman's eldest son, Mustafa.

Hürrem didn't want her sons to fight, and she used her influence to ensure Suleyman chose Selim as his heir. Sadly, Hürrem didn't live to see him crowned as the Sultan. She died in 1558, eight years before Suleyman. Upon Suleyman's death, Selim became the Sultan and so one of Hürrem's children ruled long after she died.

Nur Jahan
The refugee Empress

Nur Jahan was the most powerful woman of the mighty Mughal Empire in India, which began in 1526 and ended in 1857 when the British Empire took over. As the wife of the fourth Emperor Jahangir, she ruled in his name with his blessing. Nur Jahan's story is one of family loyalties and political greed. Her dream was for her children to rule India, and she was ready to do anything to make that happen.

Her story begins as a refugee travelling into India with her family in hope of a better life.

The baby girl's cries rang out across the desert. She was hungry, but more than that she was thirsty. The hot sun was beating down on five figures as they trudged through the sand. The father, Mirza Ghiyas Beg, the mother, Asmat Begum, their two young boys, Asaf and Muhammed Sharif, and their baby girl. They only had two mules and had to take turns riding them.

Asmat took out her water flask and shook it. There were only a few drops left.

"Save the water for later," Mirza Ghiyas muttered, as he guided the mule forward. He was

so parched that his lips had cracked, and white foam had gathered at the corners of his mouth.

"She needs it now," Asmat said, unfastening the flask to tip the drops into the baby's mouth. It wasn't enough and she cried for more. Asmat rocked the baby against her chest and tried to soothe her with a lullaby, but the baby screamed and screamed. Eventually, exhausted, her head tipped back and she fell into a deep sleep.

"We should have left her in Kandahar," Mirza Ghiyas said. "Someone would have taken her in."

"I couldn't do it," Asmat sobbed, cradling her baby close.

The family had fled Isfahan in around 1576. Their Iranian homeland was no longer safe as they had fallen out of favour with the ruling royal family, and needed to move as far away as possible. Mirza Ghiyas had chosen the Mughal Empire's capital, Agra, in India. Emperor Akbar's court was said to be welcoming to those who were eager to make their fortune. People from all over the world went to trade there, and the culture of music and art was expanding.

Mirza Ghiyas was sad to leave his homeland. He came from a noble family, which was why his name carried the title of "Mirza", meaning "noble-born". His grandfather had been the Wazir, the Prime Minister of Isfahan, and extremely close to the ruling Shah – the Persian title for "King". It was a tragedy they no longer had their comfortable, happy life.

With his wife pregnant again, Mirza had stacked his mules with supplies for the long journey to India. Unfortunately, they were not even halfway through their journey when bandits attacked them and stole their supplies and money.

They were left with only two mules, but the family of four managed to get to the closest town. It was there in Kandahar that their baby was born.

Mirza Ghiyas had gazed at the baby girl and wondered how they would take her across the rough terrain and then the desert to India. He was afraid that she wouldn't survive, and they would have to bury her in an unknown spot that they would never be able to visit again.

Mirza felt that it would be best to leave his daughter in Kandahar. Someone would adopt her, he thought, and she would grow up and have a life of her own.

Asmat didn't agree. What if their baby was mistreated or starved? Her daughter would take her chance on the road just like the rest of them.

And so the family of five had set off. They'd been on the road for so long, Asmat didn't know how many days had passed. Had the family been walking for weeks, or was it months? If they didn't get water from an outpost soon, the sand would surely swallow them up and no one would even notice.

"How much further?" Asmat mumbled.

"Just a little bit more," Mirza Ghiyas replied.

"What's that over there?" Asaf cried, pointing to a line of horses and carts.

"It's a **caravan** of travellers," Mirza Ghiyas said. "Let's ask if we can join them."

The travellers looked at the baby in Asmat's arms and agreed they could join them. The family joined the trail, content that they'd be safe for the rest of the journey.

"See, babies bring their own fortune," Asmat said. "Our little arrival has changed ours."

The baby girl, Mehr-Un-Nissa, gurgled.

When they arrived in Agra, Mirza Ghiyas Beg's name and reputation enabled him to find a job working in the court of Emperor Akbar.

As an honest and capable official, he was soon promoted to the position of finance minister and was able to provide a very good life for his family. Mehr-Un-Nissa, along with her brothers, was given the best education. She could speak Persian and Arabic, and learnt about art, books, music and dance.

In 1594, when Mehr-Un-Nissa was 17, Emperor Akbar arranged for her to be married to a Persian soldier called Sher Afghan Khan. Sher Afghan had fought in military campaigns for Emperor Akbar for many years, and had been rewarded for his bravery with a position at the royal court. They had a baby daughter called Ladli, and Mehr-Un-Nissa was happy with her comfortable life.

The Emperor Akbar's reign had been successful, and he was enjoying his old age. His son and heir, Jahangir, however, was restless to take over as ruler. He'd tried to overthrow his father, but Akbar had learnt about the treason and stopped it. Sher Afghan supported Emperor Akbar, and didn't understand Jahangir's impatience. Akbar wouldn't live forever. All Jahangir had to do was wait. True enough, Akbar died in 1605, and Jahangir became the Emperor. He took revenge on all those who had worked against him, like Sher Afghan.

Jahangir never fully trusted Sher Afghan and, in 1607, he was killed by Jahangir's men. Some believed that Jahangir ordered the killing, but no one knew for sure. Mehr-Un-Nissa found herself a young widow, but it was the practice of the royal court to invite widows to live in the palace as ladies-in-waiting. This meant they had a job and somewhere safe to live.

Mehr-Un-Nissa was soon appointed as lady-in-waiting to the chief wife of Emperor Akbar and Jahangir's foster mother, Ruqaiya Sultan Begum. For four years, she served the **Empress Dowager** and the two enjoyed a great friendship. Mehr-Un-Nissa also became a skilled polo player and played with the other women and princesses of the court.

In 1611, during the spring festival, Emperor Jahangir saw Mehr-Un-Nissa in the palace grounds and fell in love with her on sight. He proposed marriage and Mehr-Un-Nissa became the Emperor's twentieth and last wife.

As Empress, Mehr-Un-Nissa was given a new title, Nur Jahan, which means "Light of the World". The Emperor trusted her completely and insisted that all matters of state had to be passed by her. This meant that Nur Jahan was the most powerful person in the Mughal Empire after the Emperor. She persuaded her husband to give powerful positions to her father and brothers.

Her father became the Prime Minister of the Mughal Empire, and her brother Asaf held the position of **Grand Vizier** to the Emperor, as well as being a military commander.

There were many who resented the concentration of power within the same family. Some whispered horrible stories about Nur Jahan but she didn't let them affect her. Instead, she enjoyed her power and position. Her favourite thing to do was go hunting with Jahangir and she was given the nickname "Tiger Slayer" for her success at hunting tigers.

Slowly over the years, Jahangir withdrew from public life; he became ill and preferred to remain in his chambers. He completely trusted his wife to run the empire. Nur Jahan had coins made with her title stamped on them and she wondered how her name could live on forever.

Nur Jahan wanted a son who could be the next emperor. She knew she could have persuaded Jahangir to name any son they had as his heir but, as the years passed, she realised Ladli, the daughter she had with her first husband, would be her only child. Nur Jahan knew that a woman could only secure power and success through marriage to a man during these times and in this land. Therefore, if her Ladli married one of Jahangir's five sons, one of *their* children might become emperor.

"Ladli," Nur Jahan said, stroking her daughter's long, luxurious hair. They were sitting by the water fountain in the summer heat. "I want you to spend time with Prince Khurram. It's widely known that he is the Emperor's favourite son, and may be chosen as his heir."

"What should I do?" Ladli asked.

"Let him notice you," Nur Jahan replied.

Ladli bit her lip nervously. "I shall try."

"No, you shall not try!" Nur Jahan snapped. "You shall do it. My father arrived in this country as a refugee. Do you think we rose to the very top of the Mughal Empire by trying? No, we didn't just try. We set out every day with a goal and took steps to make it happen."

"Yes, Mother," Ladli mumbled.

That evening, Nur Jahan watched Jahangir's sons at dinner. Ladli was dressed in a beautiful rose shade and was wearing jewels which Jahangir had given to her as a gift. The diamonds sparkled on Ladli's neck, ears and wrists as she moved gracefully around Prince Khurram. To Nur Jahan's dismay, Prince Khurram seemed to only have eyes for her brother Asaf's daughter, Arjumund.

Nur Jahan loved her niece very much, but she loved her daughter more. Her eyes narrowed as she observed the way the prince and Arjumund ignored Ladli even though she was standing beside them.

If Nur Jahan had learnt anything as an empress with ruling power, it was that if one plan failed, there could always be another. Prince Khurram wasn't Jahangir's only son. He might be her husband's favourite now, but Nur Jahan could soon change that. She glanced around at his other sons. Which one would be suitable for Ladli?

By suitable, Nur Jahan meant which one could she control. Her eyes stopped on Jahangir's youngest son, handsome Prince Shahryar. *Hmm,* she thought, *perhaps he would do.* Nur Jahan turned back towards Ladli and indicated for her to approach. Ladli practically ran to her side, so eager was she to get away from Prince Khurram and Arjumund.

"I tried – " Ladli blurted out.

Nur Jahan held up a hand to stroke her daughter's cheek. "Hush," she soothed. "I saw it all. There are plenty more princes in the sea. Look over there, can you see Prince Shahryar?"

Ladli swallowed and nodded.

"He's the one," Nur Jahan whispered. "Now go and catch him."

Nur Jahan's planning worked. By 1621, Prince Shahryar and Ladli were married – their wedding was a magnificent affair in the Mughal court. Now it was time to set her next plan in motion.

Nur Jahan sat by Jahangir's side under the moonlit sky. "The rebel lands in the south require a strong hand," she told him. "The rebels are getting out of control and a Mughal prince should be sent to bring the place to order. I think Prince Khurram should go. He reminds me so much of you, so strong and able, and he would be best suited for this task."

Jahangir was always unaware of Nur Jahan's manipulation. "Do whatever you think is right," he said. "You have my blessing."

A few days later, Prince Khurram scowled down at his stepmother. "I know you're trying to keep me away from my father," he spat.

Nur Jahan smiled innocently. "Why would I do that? You are a prince, and the empire requires you to do your duty."

"I'll do my duty, and I'll be back," Prince Khurram vowed.

"Take your time," Nur Jahan muttered under her breath, as she turned away.

With Prince Khurram removed from court, Nur Jahan set out to convince Jahangir to name Shahryar as his heir. But for once, Jahangir didn't listen to his wife.

"My beloved, it wouldn't be right for me to name him heir," Jahangir said. "My sons must fight it out among themselves, and the strongest and most cunning will win the Emperor's throne. That's the only way the empire will survive."

Nur Jahan didn't give up. She kept telling Jahangir that Shahryar should be his heir, and she kept ruling on Jahangir's behalf.

Away from court, Prince Khurram became restless for power. He believed that Nur Jahan was poisoning his father against him and he decided to rebel against the Emperor. He led his own army of soldiers against Jahangir, but he was defeated by the Emperor's forces, who were highly trained and organised.

For years, Prince Khurram stayed away from the royal court, afraid of his father's anger. Jahangir, however, was getting old and, although it had broken his heart when his son had rebelled against him, the Emperor decided that he would forgive him. Nur Jahan tried to persuade the Emperor against it, but Jahangir wouldn't listen. After all, hadn't he done the same thing when his father was emperor, and hadn't Emperor Akbar forgiven him?

"Sons make mistakes and fathers forgive them," Nur Jahan muttered bitterly when Prince Khurram returned to the royal court.

Nur Jahan didn't just sit back and allow Prince Khurram to make up for lost time at the court. She ordered him to another far-away part of the empire to handle another rebellion. This time, Prince Khurram didn't argue. He packed his bags and off he went, taking his wife, Arjumund, and children with him. Nur Jahan felt that her son-in-law Shahryar needed experience of being a leader, so she sent him to become the governor of Lahore.

By 1626, Nur Jahan and Jahangir had been married for 15 years. They were still very much in love and Jahangir relied increasingly on his wife. Nur Jahan's love and loyalty was soon put to the test. When Jahangir travelled to Kashmir, rebels led by one of his commanders surrounded his party and took him captive. The news was brought to Nur Jahan early one morning. She paced the palace floor while the empire's generals stood in line waiting for her command.

"We'll rescue the Emperor ourselves," she declared.

"We?" the Chief General repeated.

"Yes, I shall ride into battle on top of an elephant!" Nur Jahan declared.

"But, Your Highness, that wouldn't be wise," the Chief General objected. "Leave it with us. We will crush the rebels and – "

Nur Jahan held up a hand. "No! I shall rescue my husband."

And so, the Mughal army with Nur Jahan leading on an elephant set off to rescue the Emperor. But the rebels were prepared and the soldiers that surrounded her elephant were killed. Nur Jahan was captured and placed in the same cell as the Emperor. She hugged her husband and told him not to worry.

"My plan was to get captured so I could be with you," she whispered in his ear. "And now we'll escape together."

Jahangir hugged his wife tightly. He loved her bravery and intellect so much.

Nur Jahan began to talk to some of the guards and convinced them to switch sides. She promised to reward them with riches if they swore allegiance to her husband. Many were persuaded by the Empress's words, and soon released

Jahangir and Nur Jahan. They even joined
Nur Jahan and Jahangir's counter-attack against
the main rebel leader.

Now victorious and free, Jahangir and
Nur Jahan returned to their palace.

The following year, Jahangir died. Nur Jahan was
devastated; she'd loved him dearly and loved the
power he'd given her. But as she sat receiving
mourners at his funeral, Nur Jahan's expression
hardened. She had no time to grieve her husband.
He'd died without naming an heir and she knew
that his five sons would now fight each other to
become the emperor. Her power had died with
her husband, but she needed to ensure that her
son-in-law, Shahryar, became the emperor.

Nur Jahan had taught Shahryar well. Over in
Lahore, he declared himself to be the emperor
and, for a short while, Nur Jahan believed
they'd succeeded in securing the throne for her
bloodline. It was not to be.

Nur Jahan was caught totally by surprise when her brother Asaf stormed into her quarters with soldiers and arrested her.

"Why?" Nur Jahan demanded. "Why are you doing this?"

"You want your daughter on the throne," he said, in a low voice. "But I want *my* daughter on the throne."

"Brother Asaf," Nur Jahan begged. "Please don't do this. Shahryar has already declared himself Emperor. If he's challenged, there will only be bloodshed."

"Be that as it may," Asaf replied, turning to his soldiers. "Take her away."

Nur Jahan remained locked up until the new emperor had been declared. Days passed and, when she was finally released, Nur Jahan asked one of the maids who the emperor was.

"Prince Khurram," the maid replied.

"And what happened to Shahryar?" Nur Jahan asked, but she already knew the answer.

"Asaf Khan sent the Mughal army to challenge Prince Shahryar," the maid said. "Prince Shahryar's army was defeated, and Prince Khurram raced back to court and was declared the Emperor. Prince Shahryar is dead."

Nur Jahan closed her eyes. She'd loved the prince as her son. He had made her daughter happy and now Ladli was a widow, just like she'd been when Sher Afghan had been killed. Nur Jahan had rebuilt her life at the palace when she had worked as lady-in-waiting and then Jahangir had made her his beloved wife. Would Ladli get another chance at happiness? Or would she be shunned as the widow of the prince who was defeated?

Nur Jahan soon found out.

Prince Khurram ordered his stepmother be placed under house arrest far away from court; he didn't want her scheming against him. Nur Jahan, Ladli and her children were sent to live in a house in Lahore. Then Prince Khurram gave himself the title Shah Jahan, which means "King of the World". His wife Arjumund was given the title Mumtaz Mahal, which means "beloved **ornament** of the palace."

Nur Jahan never returned to the royal court, and spent the rest of her life in Lahore. A few years after her exile she learnt that Arjumund had died.

"They say that Khurram is building a tomb for Arjumund, and it's based on the model you designed for grandfather's tomb," Ladli said.

Nur Jahan wasn't interested in what the Emperor was building for his dead wife. Or that the design was like the one she'd made for her father, Mirza Ghiyas.

"They claim that it'll be the most beautiful building in the world and people from all corners of the earth will come to see it," Ladli continued. "I hear it will be made of white marble and have a dome and four minarets."

"What will he call it?" Nur Jahan asked.

"The Taj Mahal."

Rani Lakshmibai, Hürrem and Nur Jahan were from ordinary families. No one could have imagined that those little girls would grow up to become powerful queens – remembered by their people for their strong leadership.

Faced with obstacles, challenges and men who didn't approve of so much power in a woman's hands, they didn't back down. They were intelligent, charming, brave and fierce. Whether they were in a palace or on the battlefield, they fought for what they believed in.

Rani Lakshmibai's stand for freedom helped bring an end to the mighty East India Company. Hürrem helped the poor and began the **Sultanate of Women**. Nur Jahan ruled in her husband's name and was once the most powerful person in the mighty Mughal Empire.

All are worthy of the title Queen.

Glossary

caravan a group of people, especially traders, travelling together across a desert in Asia or North Africa.

Constantinople modern-day Istanbul

Empress Dowager mother or widow of an emperor

Grand Vizier title given to the highest-ranking government minister

haseki special, or someone who belongs to a ruler

military campaigns large-scale, long-term coordinated battles

Mughal Empire an area that covered most of modern-day India, Pakistan and Afghanistan

ornament something beautiful

Ottoman Empire at its height in the 16th century, covered large areas of southeastern Europe, northern Africa and the Middle East

Persia modern-day Iran

Queen Mother widow of a king, and mother of the monarch

Sultanate of Women a period of about 130 years, from 1533, when women connected to the Sultan had political powers

Book talk questions

What are the main characteristics of Lakshmibai's personality?

What would you do if you had Hürrem's power?

How did Nur Jahan use her wits to get what she wanted?

What was the role of the East India Company in Lakshmibai's story?

How do you think Roxelana would want to be remembered?

What lessons can we learn from Nur Jahan's life that apply to us today?

What makes a good leader?

What challenges do you think women faced throughout history?

Which other women from history do you admire?

In your opinion, which person from the modern day will be remembered forever?

Ask the author

What inspires you to write for children?
I've always loved reading stories and, the more I read, the more I want to create my own stories. If I've enjoyed a history book, I want to recreate that period in a children's story.

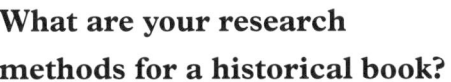
Sufiya Ahmed

What are your research methods for a historical book?
I read a lot of adult non-fiction history books, so I can imagine the settings for my stories and also to understand why historical figures behaved the way they did. It helps when I'm creating characters.

What part of this book did you enjoy writing the most?
The parts when the three queens stood up to all the men who thought they shouldn't have power.

Which other female figures would you like to write about?
Razia Sultan – an Indian queen of the 13th century.

Who are your biggest influences as a writer?
I'm a writer because I was a reader first; my two favourite childhood authors were Enid Blyton and Roald Dahl. They inspired me to become a writer.

How do you think your background influences your writing?
I am British with South Asian heritage, and I like to write about events and figures that are not always included in children's history books. I grew up with the legend of Rani Lakshmibai and her defiance. I also remember first learning about Nur Jahan on a trip to see the Taj Mahal when I was 12. My father bought me a children's book on the Mughal Empire so I could have knowledge about all the historical sites we were visiting.

What is your favourite historical period?
The last 1,000 years starting from 1066 and all the empires of the world that have ruled up to the Second World War.

What do you like to do in your free time?
Curling up with a book is still my favourite thing to do.

Published by Collins
An imprint of HarperCollins*Publishers*

The News Building
1 London Bridge Street
London SE1 9GF
UK

Macken House
39/40 Mayor Street Upper
Dublin 1
D01 C9W8
Ireland

© HarperCollins*Publishers* Limited 2026

10 9 8 7 6 5 4 3 2 1

ISBN 978-0-00-878478-2

All rights reserved. No part of this publication may be reproduced, stored in a retrieval system, or transmitted in any form by any means, electronic, mechanical, photocopying, recording or otherwise, without the prior written permission of the Publisher or a licence permitting restricted copying in the United Kingdom issued by the Copyright Licensing Agency Ltd, 5th Floor, Shackleton House, 4 Battle Bridge Lane, London SE1 2HX.

Without limiting the exclusive rights of any author, contributor or the publisher of this publication, any unauthorised use of this publication to train generative artificial intelligence (AI) technologies is expressly prohibited. HarperCollins also exercise their rights under Article 4(3) of the Digital Single Market Directive 2019/790 and expressly reserve this publication from the text and data mining exception.

British Library Cataloguing-in-Publication Data
A catalogue record for this publication is available from the British Library.

Author: Sufiya Ahmed
Illustrator: Markia Jenai (Astound Agency)
Publisher: Laura White
Commissioning editor: Holly Woolnough
Development editor: Zoë Clarke
Product manager: Holly Woolnough
Content editor: Selin Akca
Copyeditor: Sally Byford

Proofreaders: Tanya Solomons, Sasha Morton
Reviewer: Lisa Davis
Fact checker: Sally Byford
Cover designer: Sarah Finan
Internal designer: 2Hoots Publishing Services Ltd
Typesetter: David Jimenez
Production controller: Sophie Waeland

Collins would like to thank the teachers and children at Grange Primary School, Southwark, for being part of the development of Big Cat Read On.

Printed in the UK

MIX
Paper | Supporting responsible forestry
FSC® C006032

Made with responsibly sourced paper and vegetable ink

Scan to see how we are reducing our environmental impact.

Get the latest Collins Big Cat news at
collins.co.uk/collinsbigcat